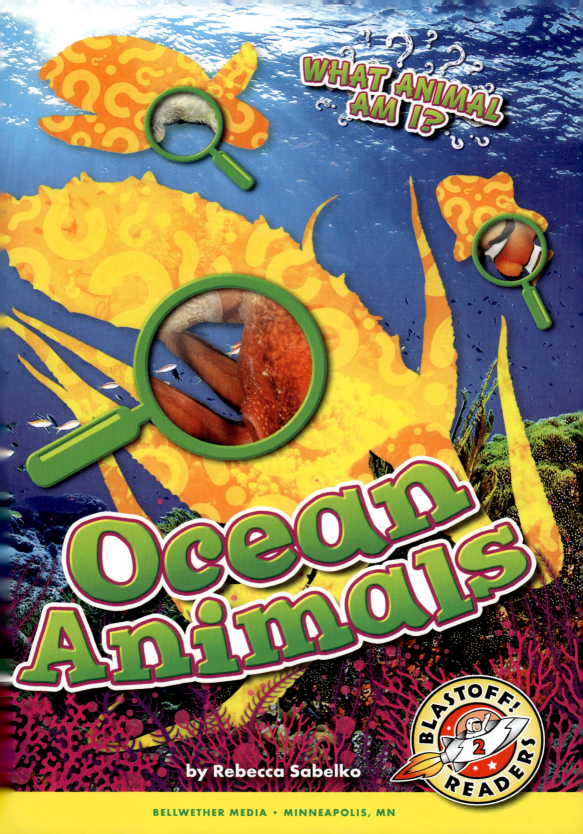

Blastoff! Readers are carefully developed by literacy experts to build reading stamina and move students toward fluency by combining standards-based content with developmentally appropriate text.

Level 1 provides the most support through repetition of high-frequency words, light text, predictable sentence patterns, and strong visual support.

Level 2 offers early readers a bit more challenge through varied sentences, increased text load, and text-supportive special features.

Level 3 advances early-fluent readers toward fluency through increased text load, less reliance on photos, advancing concepts, longer sentences, and more complex special features.

★ **Blastoff! Universe**

 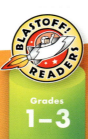 

Reading Level: Grade K (Blastoff! Beginners) → Grades 1–3 (Blastoff! Readers) → Grade 4 (Blastoff! Discovery)

This edition first published in 2023 by Bellwether Media, Inc.

No part of this publication may be reproduced in whole or in part without written permission of the publisher. For information regarding permission, write to Bellwether Media, Inc., Attention: Permissions Department, 6012 Blue Circle Drive, Minnetonka, MN 55343.

Library of Congress Cataloging-in-Publication Data

Names: Sabelko, Rebecca, author.
Title: Ocean animals / by Rebecca Sabelko.
Description: Minneapolis, MN : Bellwether Media, Inc., [2023] | Series: What animal am I? | Includes bibliographical references and index. | Audience: Ages 5-8 | Audience: Grades 2-3 | Summary: "Relevant images match informative text in this introduction to different ocean animals. Intended for students in kindergarten through third grade" -- Provided by publisher.
Identifiers: LCCN 2022009386 (print) | LCCN 2022009387 (ebook) | ISBN 9781644877302 (library binding) | ISBN 9781648347764 (ebook)
Subjects: LCSH: Marine animals--Juvenile literature.
Classification: LCC QL122.2 .S233 2023 (print) | LCC QL122.2 (ebook) | DDC 591.77--dc23/eng/20220303
LC record available at https://lccn.loc.gov/2022009386
LC ebook record available at https://lccn.loc.gov/2022009387

Text copyright © 2023 by Bellwether Media, Inc. BLASTOFF! READERS and associated logos are trademarks and/or registered trademarks of Bellwether Media, Inc.

Editor: Rachael Barnes   Designer: Brittany McIntosh

Printed in the United States of America, North Mankato, MN.

Table of Contents

Welcome to the Ocean!	4
An Ocean Giant	6
A Rubber-shelled Reptile	10
A Color Changer	14
An Anemone's Friend	18
Glossary	22
To Learn More	23
Index	24

Welcome to the Ocean!

Oceans are huge bodies of salt water. They cover most of Earth's surface.

Around one million animal **species** live in oceans!

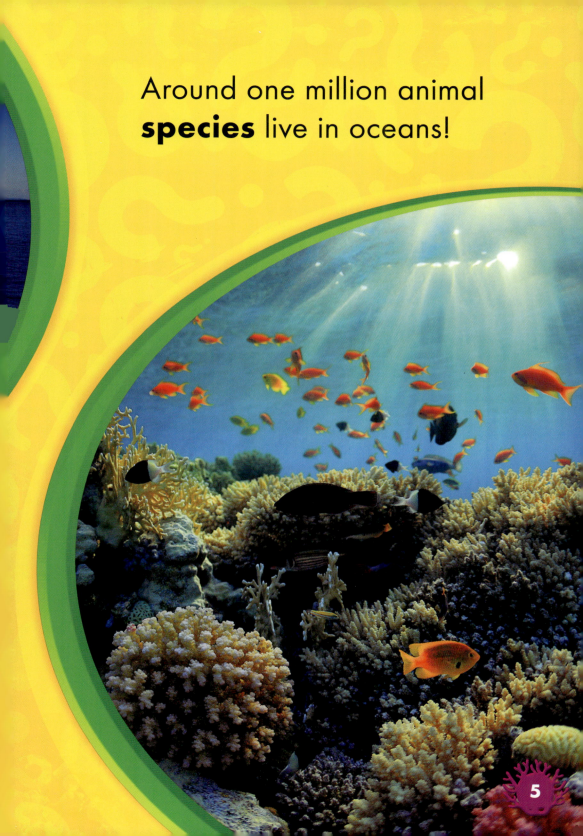

An Ocean Giant

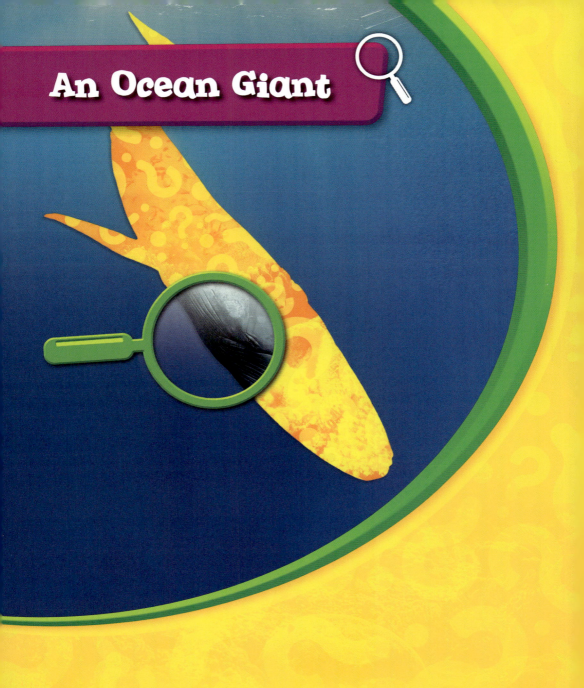

I am the largest **mammal** on Earth! I have a bluish-gray body.

I breathe air through my **blowholes**. What animal am I?

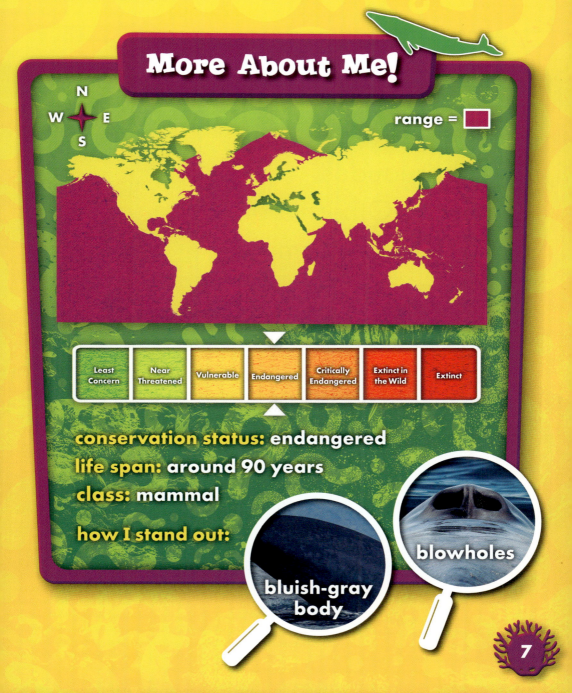

More About Me!

range =

conservation status: endangered
life span: around 90 years
class: mammal
how I stand out: bluish-gray body, blowholes

I am a blue whale! I live in every ocean except the Arctic Ocean.

I am one of the world's loudest animals. Other whales can hear me from miles away!

Blue Whale Food

krill

A Rubber-shelled Reptile

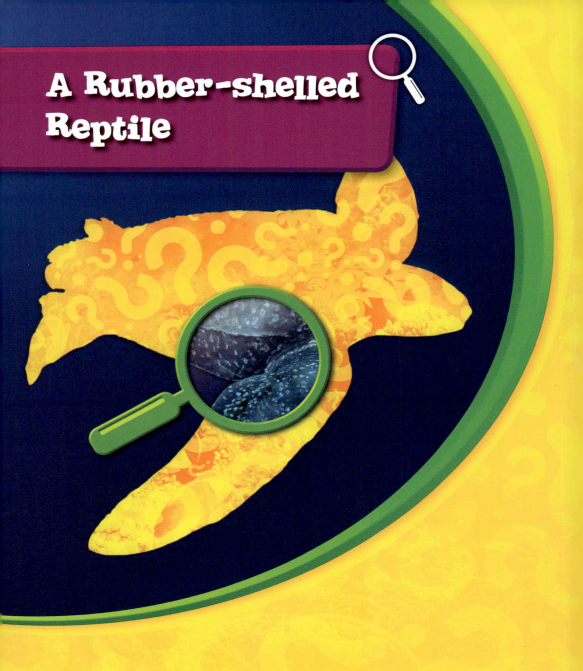

I am a **reptile**. My black shell is **flexible** and rubbery.

My long front **flippers** help me move through water. What animal am I?

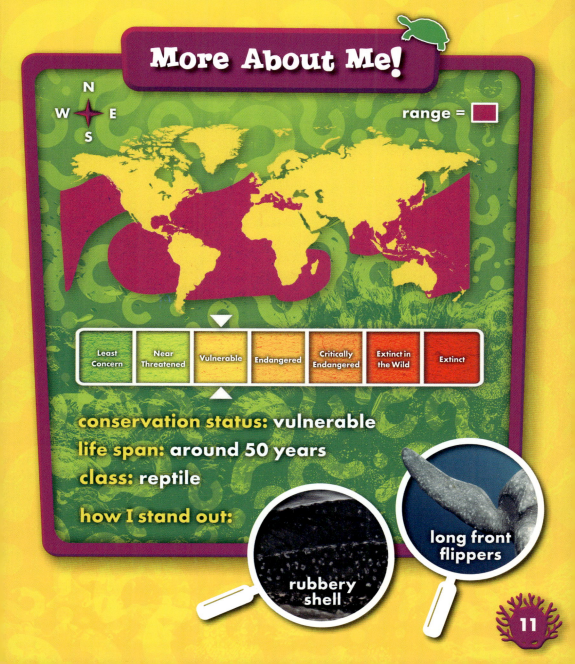

More About Me!

range =

Least Concern | Near Threatened | Vulnerable | Endangered | Critically Endangered | Extinct in the Wild | Extinct

conservation status: vulnerable
life span: around 50 years
class: reptile
how I stand out:

rubbery shell

long front flippers

Leatherback Sea Turtle Food

jellyfish

eggs

I am a leatherback sea turtle! I mostly eat jellyfish.

I make long **migrations** to warm beaches. I lay eggs in the sand.

A Color Changer

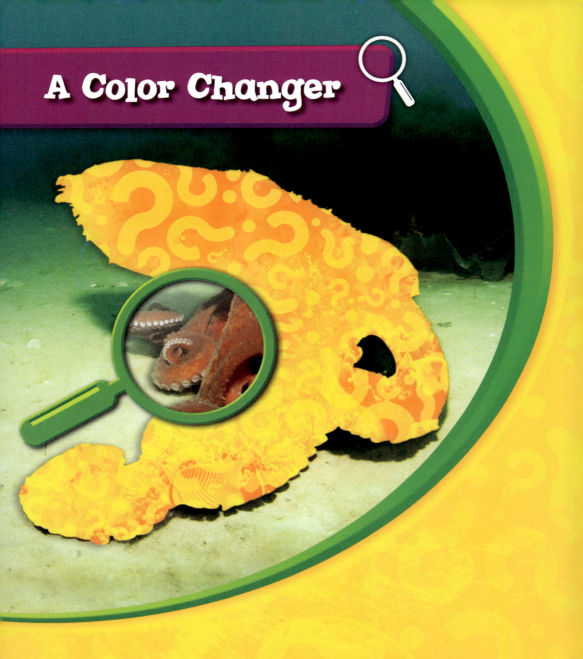

I am an **invertebrate**.
My bulb-shaped body is flexible!

I have a reddish-brown body. But I can change colors to blend in. What animal am I?

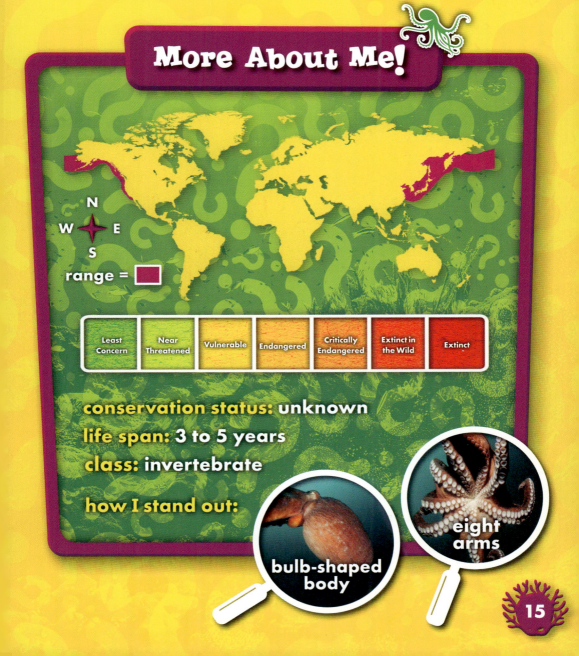

More About Me!

range =

| Least Concern | Near Threatened | Vulnerable | Endangered | Critically Endangered | Extinct in the Wild | Extinct |

conservation status: unknown
life span: 3 to 5 years
class: invertebrate
how I stand out:

bulb-shaped body

eight arms

I am a giant Pacific octopus! Eight arms help me move.

I hunt at night. My beak-like mouth tears food to pieces!

Giant Pacific Octopus Food

clams   fish   shrimp

An Anemone's Friend

I am a bright orange fish with three white stripes.

I live in warm waters around Australia and southern Asia. What animal am I?

More About Me!

range =

Least Concern | Near Threatened | Vulnerable | Endangered | Critically Endangered | Extinct in the Wild | Extinct

conservation status: unknown

life span: 6 to 10 years

class: fish

how I stand out: bright orange, white stripes

Common Clownfish Food

algae

zooplankton

sea anemone

I am a common clownfish! I live in **sea anemones**. They keep me safe from enemies.

I eat **algae**. I live well in my ocean home!

Glossary

algae—plants and plantlike living things; most kinds of algae grow in water.

blowholes—the holes on top of a blue whale's head that are used for breathing

flexible—bendable

flippers—wide, flat body parts that are used for swimming

invertebrate—an animal without a backbone

mammal—a warm-blooded animal that has a backbone and feeds its young milk

migrations—travels from one place to another, often with the seasons

reptile—a cold-blooded animal that has a backbone and lays eggs

sea anemones—small, brightly colored sea animals that look like flowers and stick to rocks and coral

species—kinds of animals

To Learn More

AT THE LIBRARY

Grodzicki, Jenna. *Baby Sea Turtles*. Minneapolis, Minn.: Bearport Publishing Company, 2022.

Harris, Bizzy. *Octopuses*. Minneapolis, Minn.: Jump!, 2022.

Kenney, Karen Latchana. *Oceans*. Minneapolis, Minn.: Bellwether Media, 2022.

ON THE WEB

Factsurfer.com gives you a safe, fun way to find more information.

1. Go to www.factsurfer.com.

2. Enter "ocean animals" into the search box and click 🔍.

3. Select your book cover to see a list of related content.

Index

Arctic Ocean, 8
arms, 16
Asia, 19
Australia, 19
blowholes, 7
blue whale, 6–7, 8–9
body, 6, 14, 15
color, 6, 10, 15, 18
common clownfish, 18–19, 20–21
Earth, 4, 6
eggs, 12, 13
fish, 18
flexible, 10, 14
flippers, 11
food, 9, 12, 13, 16, 17, 20, 21
giant Pacific octopus, 14–15, 16–17
hunt, 16
invertebrate, 14
leatherback sea turtle, 10–11, 12–13
loud, 8
mammal, 6
migrations, 13
more about me, 7, 11, 15, 19
mouth, 16
night, 16
reptile, 10
sand, 13
sea anemones, 20, 21
shell, 10
size, 6
species, 5
stripes, 18
water, 4, 11, 19

The images in this book are reproduced through the courtesy of: Kondratuk Aleksei, front cover (octopus), p. 15 (left); Rich Carey, front cover (turtle); Kletr, front cover (clownfish), p. 19 (left); Irina Markova, front cover (background); Seashell World, p. 3; Dudarev Mikhail, p. 4; Borisoff, p. 5; WaterFrame/ Alamy, pp. 6, 8-9; Johan_R, p. 7 (left); BIOSPHOTO/ Alamy, p. 7 (right); Chase Dekker, p. 8; RLS Photo, p. 9 (top); Michael Patrick O'Neill/ Alamy, p. 10; Stephanie Rousseau, p. 11 (left); Doug Perrine/ Alamy, p. 11 (right); Beautiful landscape, p. 12 (top); frans lemmens/ Alamy, pp. 12-13; Lynsey Allan, p. 12 (bottom); Steve Bloom Images/ Alamy, p. 13; Konstantin Novikov, pp. 14, 15 (right); Kondratuk Aleksei, p. 15 (left); Pete Niesen/ Alamy, p. 16; All Canada Photos/ Alamy, pp. 16-17; optimarc, p. 17 (top left); Design Pics Inc/ Alamy, p. 17 (top middle); Bill Kennedy, p. 17 (top right); Artur Arantes Fh, p. 18; Alex Stemmers, p. 19 (right); Richard Whitcombe, p. 20 (top left); Choksawatdikorn, p. 20 (top right); blue-sea.cz, pp. 20-21; DiveIvanov, p. 21; Potapov Alexander, pp. 22, 23.